Events of 1931

News for every day of the year

The Round Table Conference between the British government and Indian nationalists in London on 14 September 1931. Mahatma Gandhi is seated centre right.

By Hugh Morrison

MONTPELIER PUBLISHING

Front cover (clockwise from left): Charlie Chaplin and Virginia Cherrill in *City Lights*. Mahatma Gandhi. Poster for *The Public Enemy* starring James Cagney and Jean Harlow. The Ford Model A.

Back cover (clockwise from top): Poster for *Little Caesar* starring Edward G Robinson and Glenda Farrell. The new Empire State building. The Australian tennis star, Coral Buttsworth. Poster for *Frankenstein* starring Colin Clive and Boris Karloff. Hattie Caraway, the first female US Senator. Britain's R100 airship.

Image credits: Eva Rinaldi, Chris McAndrew, HIHI2020, Carl Lender, Agence de Presse Meurisse, Bain News Service, United States Coast Guard, Miami Police Department, Gustavo Facci, Richard Smith.

January
1931

Thursday 1: Britain's Road Traffic Act 1930 comes into force. Speed limits are abolished, but drink-driving and driving without insurance become illegal.

Friday 2: Florencio Harmodio Arosemena, President of Panama, is overthrown and imprisoned by a military junta.

Saturday 3: The film *The Criminal Code* starring Walter Huston is released.

The French Great War leader Marshal Joffre dies aged 78.

Sunday 4: HRH Princess Louise, the Princess Royal (sister of HM King George V) dies aged 63.

Monday 5: Actor and director Robert Duvall (*To Kill a Mockingbird, M.A.S.H.*) is born in San Diego, California.

Tuesday 6: The novelist E L Doctorow (*Ragtime*) is born in New York City (died 2015).

London's rebuilt Sadlers Wells Theatre opens.

January 1931

Wednesday 7: The funeral of France's Marshal Joffre takes place at Notre Dame Cathedral in Paris.

Thursday 8: New York City's Newark airport becomes the busiest in the world, with traffic surpassing that of London's Croydon Aerodrome.

Friday 9: A large scale Prohibition raid takes place on hotels in the small Nevada town of Las Vegas, which are suspected of serving liquor to workers on the nearby Hoover Dam.

HRH Princess Louise the Princess Royal, (shown here in 1901), dies on 4 January.

Saturday 10: HRH the Prince of Wales (later King Edward VIII) is introduced to Wallis Simpson at a house party at Burrough Court, Melton Mowbray. The King's engagement to the twice-divorced Mrs Simpson leads to his abdication in 1936.

Sunday 11: Five prisoners escape from the state penitentiary at Santa Fe, New Mexico, after digging a 30 yard tunnel.

Monday 12: Raymond Gunn, 27, is killed by a lynch mob in Maryville, Missouri, after confessing to the murder of a local schoolmistress.

Tuesday 13: Marie Kordos is hanged in Hungary for her part in a mass poisoning of up to 300 people in the village of Nagyrev between 1911 and 1929.

Wednesday 14: Singer Caterina Valente is born in Paris, France.

Thursday 15: 11 Italian seaplanes led by Italo Balbo arrive in Brazil after a 6000 mile flight that began on 17 December.

Friday 16: Ricardo Joaquín Alfaro Jované becomes President of Panama.

Saturday 17: The actor James Earl Jones (famous for Darth Vader's voice in *Star Wars*) is born in Arkabutla, Mississippi.

Sunday 18: President Paul von Hindenburg addresses a crowd of 12,000 in Berlin on the 60th anniversary of the German Empire.

Monday 19: London's first Round Table Conference ends with British PM Ramsay Macdonald offering to grant Dominion status to India, on a par with Australia and Canada.

Actor James Earl Jones is born on 17 January.

Tuesday 20: The report of the Wickersham Commission on US prohibition recommends that the ban on alcohol should continue.

Wednesday 21: Britain's House of Commons votes not to extend the school leaving age from 14 to 15.

Thursday 22: Singer-songwriter Sam Cooke (*Chain Gang, Twistin' the Night Away*) is born (died 1964).

Friday 23: The Russian ballerina Anna Pavlova dies in exile in Golders Green, London, aged 49.

Saturday 24: A survey by the Metropolitan Life Insurance Company estimates that 4.5 million Americans are out of work.

Britain's Prime Minister Ramsay Macdonald.

January 1931

Sunday 25: The gangster film *Little Caesar* starring Edward G Robinson and Douglas Fairbanks Jr is released in the USA.

Monday 26: Britain's future Prime Minister Winston Churchill resigns from the shadow cabinet over the decision to grant Dominion status to India, claiming it will lead to religious conflict.

Tuesday 27: Pierre Laval becomes Prime Minister of France.

Wednesday 28: 28 miners are killed in a mine explosion at Linton, Indiana.

Thursday 29: 27 miners are killed in an explosion at Whitehaven, England.

Friday 30: The Charlie Chaplin comedy film *City Lights* is released in the USA.

Saturday 31: The legendary baseball player Ernie 'Mr Sunshine' Banks is born in Dallas, Texas (died 2015).

Charlie Chaplin and Virginia Cherrill star in *City Lights*.

February
1931

Sunday 1: Mahatma Gandhi and the Indian National Congress vote to continue their campaign of civil disobedience against British rule in India.

Monday 2: The comedian Les Dawson is born in Collyhurst, Manchester (died 1993).

Tuesday 3: 256 people are killed in an earthquake in Hawke's Bay, New Zealand, in what remains the country's deadliest natural disaster.

Wednesday 4: Nine RAF crewmen are killed when a Blackburn Iris flying boat crashes in the English Channel.

Thursday 5: The British racer Major Sir Malcolm Campbell sets the world land speed record at 245 mph in *Bluebird* at Daytona Beach, Florida.

Friday 6: The actor Rip Torn is born in Temple, Texas (died 2019).

English cricketer Fred Trueman is born in Stainton, Yorkshire (died 2006).

Malcolm Campbell.

February 1931

Saturday 7: Aviator Amelia Earheart marries publisher George P Putman in Noank, Connecticut.

Sunday 8: Canada wins the Fifth World Ice Hockey Championships in Poland.

Actor James Dean is born in Marion, Indiana (died 1955).

Monday 9: The British, Australian and New Zealand Antarctic Research Expedition discovers Princess Elizabeth Land.

Tuesday 10: 107 Nazi Party representatives walk out in objection to reforms of Germany's Reichstag (Parliament).

Wednesday 11: Britain's Chancellor of the Exchequer Philip Snowdon announces 'the national position is so grave that drastic and disagreeable measures will have to be taken.'

Thursday 12: Radio broadcasting begins in Japan.

Friday 13: Lord Irwin, Viceroy of India, officially proclaims New Delhi as India's capital city.

Saturday 14: The horror film *Dracula* starring Bela Lugosi in the title role is released in the USA.

Commemorative stamps for the inauguration of New Delhi.

Sunday 15: Hungary sweeps the board in the 5th World Table Tennis Championships in Budapest; England's team wins Silver.

Monday 16: The US government restricts European immigration by 90% for two years in an attempt to control unemployment.

Ozzie Nelson and his Orchestra record their hit song *Dream a Little Dream of Me.*

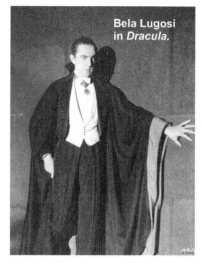

Bela Lugosi in *Dracula.*

Tuesday 17: Mahatma Gandhi holds independence talks with Lord Irwin, Viceroy of India.

Wednesday 18: The Nobel Prize winning novelist Toni Morrison (*Beloved*) is born in Lorain, Ohio (died 2019).

Thursday 19: The German musical film *The Threepenny Opera* premieres in Berlin.

Friday 20: An assassination attempt is made on King Zog of Albania at the Vienna State Opera House; he escapes unharmed.

Saturday 21: The USSR revokes the citizenship of politician Leon Trotsky, exiled for his opposition to Stalin.

Sunday 22: Three convicts are killed in an escape attempt from Illinois State Penitentiary.

Monday 23: Australian opera star Dame Nellie Melba dies aged 69.

Tuesday 24: Norwegian ski jumper Sigmund Ruud makes a world record jump of 264 feet (80.5 metres) at Davos, Switzerland.

February 1931

Sir Oswald Mosley.

Wednesday 25: Four people are killed as communist demonstrators clash with police in Germany.

Thursday 26: The film *The Skin Game*, directed by Alfred Hitchcock and based on the play by John Galsworthy, is released in the UK.

Friday 27: The *New York World* newspaper, famous for being the first to publish a crossword puzzle (in 1913), ceases publication after 71 years.

Saturday 28: The British politician Sir Oswald Mosley resigns from the Labour Party; he goes on to found the British Union of Fascists.

March
1931

Cab Calloway.

Sunday 1: Austria's Karl Schafer and Norway's Sonja Henie win the World Figure Skating Championships in Berlin.

Monday 2: Mikhail Gorbachev, last President of the USSR, is born in Privolnoye, Russia.

Tuesday 3: *The Star Spangled Banner* becomes the official national anthem of the USA, replacing *My Country 'Tis of Thee.*

Cab Calloway records his hit song *Minnie the Moocher.*

Wednesday 4: Hundreds of people are made homeless as the worst flooding since 1898 hits Boston, Massachussets.

Thursday 5: Mahatma Gandhi agrees with the Viceroy of India to end the civil disobedience campaign against British rule.

Friday 6: Ruth Rowland Nichols of New York sets the world altitude record for a woman pilot at 28,743 feet (8760.9 m).

March 1931

Saturday 7: 18 people are killed when two steamers collide during a storm on the River Danube near Belgrade, Serbia.

Sunday 8: Jack Crawford and Coral McInnes Buttsworth, both of Australia, win the Australian Tennis Championships.

Monday 9: 14 Soviet economists are imprisoned following a purge by Josef Stalin known as the Menshevik Trial.

Coral McInnes Buttsworth.

Tuesday 10: Journalist Helen Herman coins the nonsense word 'supercaliflawjalisticexpialadoshus' in the Syracuse University newspaper; it is used as the title of a song in the 1964 film *Mary Poppins.*

Wednesday 11: The newspaper magnate Rupert Murdoch is born in Melbourne, Australia.

Our Gang **actor Billie Thomas is born on 12 March.**

Thursday 12: Actor William 'Billie' Thomas, best known for playing Buckwheat in the *Our Gang/Little Rascals* comedies, is born in Los Angeles (died 1980).

Friday 13: Jewels worth over $1m are stolen from Charlton and Co's store in Palm Beach, Florida: the owner is kidnapped by the gang but later released unharmed.

Saturday 14: *Alam Ara*, the first talking picture in India, is released.

Sunday 15: 27 people are killed when the SS *Viking* explodes off the coast of Newfoundland, during the filming of the first location 'talkie', *The Viking.*

Monday 16: A Nazi Party member is killed in an attack by communists in Hamburg, Germany.

Tuesday 17: The Canadian government launches a formal complaint after the New York Coastguard fires on the vessel *Josephine K*, thought to be carrying bootleg liquor.

Star Trek **actor William Shatner is born on 22 March.**

Wednesday 18: The first modern electric razor, designed by Jacob Schick, goes on sale in the USA.

Thursday 19: The US state of Nevada legalises gambling.

Friday 20: Hermann Müller, former Chancellor of Germany, dies aged 54.

Saturday 21: Cambridge wins the 83rd Oxford v Cambridge university boat race on London's River Thames.

Sunday 22: Six people are killed when the *Royal Scot* express train derails near Leighton Buzzard, Bedfordshire, England.

The actor William Shatner (*Star Trek, TJ Hooker*) is born in Montreal, Canada.

Monday 23: Three Indian nationalists are hanged in Lahore for the murder of a British policeman and a bomb attack on the legislative assembly.

March 1931

The novelist Arnold Bennett dies on 27 March.

Tuesday 24: The Japanese parliament blocks legislation giving women the right to vote.

Wednesday 25: The US civil rights campaigner Ida B Wells dies aged 68.

Thursday 26: The actor and director Leonard Nimoy (Mr Spock in *Star Trek*) is born in Boston, Mass. (died 2015).

The Swiss national airline Swissair is founded.

Friday 27: The English novelist Arnold Bennett (*The Card, Anna of the Five Towns, Clayhanger*) dies aged 63.

Saturday 28: 12 people are killed when severe blizzards hit the Rocky Mountains, Colorado.

Sunday 29: The Indian National Congress demands nothing short of full independence from Britain.

The British Conservative politician Norman Tebbit is born in Ponders End, Middlesex.

Monday 30: Austria blames prohibition for a glut of cheap American wheat affecting European farmers.

Leonard Nimoy is born on 29 March.

Tuesday 31: The British record company EMI is founded after a merger of Columbia and His Master's Voice.

April
1931

Wednesday 1: 25 people are killed when the Royal Navy battlecruiser HMS *Glorious* collides in fog with the SS *Florida* near Gibraltar.

Thursday 2: One of the first female baseball players, Jackie Mitchell, 17, causes a sensation when she strikes out seasoned pros Babe Ruth and Lou Gehrig in a friendly in New York.

Friday 3: Martial law is declared in Managua, Nicaragua, when looting breaks out following an earthquake.

Vere Ponsonby, Governor General of Canada

Saturday 4: Vere Ponsonby, 9th Earl of Bessborough, becomes Governor General of Canada.

Sunday 5: 187 people are arrested in communist demonstrations in Berlin, Germany.

Monday 6: US spiritual guru Baba Ram Dass, author of *Be Here Now*, is born in Newton, Massachusetts (died 2019).

April 1931

Tuesday 7: The Quakers abolish their ban, in place since 1783, on the use of frills and lace in clothing.

Wednesday 8: Dimitri Shostakovich's ballet *The Bolt* premieres in Leningrad.

Thursday 9: In a landmark case, nine black youths known as the Scottsboro Boys are convicted of an attack on two white women in Tennessee. The trial is later ruled unsound and the practice of all-white juries is ended.

Friday 10: The Lebanese poet Kahlil Gibran (best known for *The Prophet*) dies aged 48.

Saturday 11: The FBI announces it has broken up one of the largest bootlegging rings in the USA, with connections stretching from Canada to British Honduras.

Sunday 12: Joe McCarthy becomes manager of the New York Yankees baseball team.

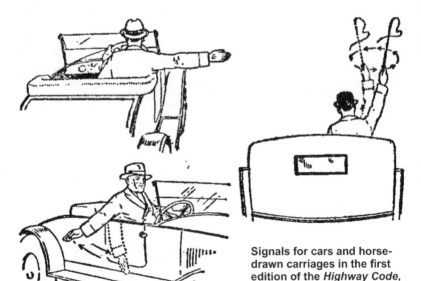

Signals for cars and horse-drawn carriages in the first edition of the *Highway Code*, published on 14 April.

Monday 13: The trial of serial killer Peter Kurten, the 'Vampire of Dusseldorf' begins in Germany.

Tuesday 14: Following a landslide victory of Republican parties across Spain, HM King Alfonso XIII goes into exile, although he does not officially abdicate.

Britain's *Highway Code* for road users is first published.

HM King Alfonso XIII of Spain.

Wednesday 15: Plennie Wingo, 36, begins the longest backwards walk on record. Using specially constructed mirror spectacles, he walks from Santa Monica to Istanbul (about 8,000 miles) in 18 months. He wears out 13 pairs of shoes on the trip.

Plennie Wingo.

Thursday 16: The exiled King Alfonso XIII of Spain is mobbed by well-wishers on his arrival in Paris.

Friday 17: The fully independent Catalan Republic, declared on 14 April, is replaced by an autonomous region within Spain.

Saturday 18: Freeman Freeman-Thomas, First Earl of Willingdon, becomes Viceroy of India.

Sunday 19: Louis Chiron of Monaco wins the 1931 Monaco Grand Prix motor race.

Monday 20: Britain's Parliament votes to allow cinemas to open on Sundays.

April 1931

James Cagney and Joan Blondell in *The Public Enemy*.

Tuesday 21: The US Navy evacuates American citizens from Paraguay following a popular uprising.

Wednesday 22: Captain Frank Hawks of Texas sets a world record when he flies from London to Rome in 5 hours 20 minutes.

Thursday 23: The gangster film *The Public Enemy,* which makes a star of James Cagney, is released.

Friday 24: The State of New York vetoes a bill enabling doctors to prescribe 'medicinal liquor'.

Saturday 25: West Bromwich Albion defeats Birmingham 2-1 in the FA (Football Association) Cup Final at Wembley Stadium, London.

Sunday 26: 3000 people are killed in the Zangezur Earthquake in Armenia/Azerbaijan.

Monday 27: Pope Pius XI attacks Benito Mussolini's Fascists, calling on them 'to be Catholics not only in name but in fact.'

Tuesday 28: A bill to abolish the death penalty in the State of California is defeated by 47 to 29 votes.

Wednesday 29: The skiffle singer Lonnie Donegan (*My Old Man's A Dustman*) is born in Glasgow (died 2002).

Thursday 30: 150 people are killed in a huge explosion at a naval bomb factory near Rio de Janeiro, Brazil.

May
1931

Friday 1: President Hoover officially opens New York City's Empire State Building, the tallest building in the world to this date.

The architectural heritage body the National Trust for Scotland is formed.

Saturday 2: A mock air raid is carried out over Toulon, France, showing military experts the devastation possible by modern bomber aircraft.

Sunday 3: The Nazi Party comes second in German state elections held in Schaumburg-Lippe.

Monday 4: Mustafa Kemel 'Ataturk' is re-elected as President of Turkey.

Tuesday 5: Three deputies and a miner are killed in a shootout during a labour dispute in Harlan County, Kentucky.

Left: the Empire State Building opens on 1 May.

May 1931

Wednesday 6: The legendary baseball player Willy Mays is born in Westfield, Alabama.

Thursday 7: The National Guard is sent to Harlan County, Kentucky, as the labour dispute in the region worsens.

Friday 8: An attempt to prosecute Adolf Hitler for complicity in a killing carried out by the Brownshirts fails.

Baseball star Willy Mays is born on 6 May.

Saturday 9: Police in Bucharest announce they have foiled an assassination plot against King Carol I of Romania.

Sunday 10: The senior Nazi Hermann Goering meets for talks with Benito Mussolini in Rome.

Peter Lorre.

Monday 11: The Fritz Lang thriller film *M*, starring Peter Lorre, premieres in Berlin.

Tuesday 12: Troops are sent to Madrid to restore order after anti-clerical rioters burn down four convents.

Wednesday 13: The International Olympic Committee announces that Berlin will host the 1936 Olympic Games.

Thursday 14: Italian conductor Arturo Toscanini is assaulted by a protestor after refusing to play *Giovinezza*, the fascist anthem, at a concert in Bologna.

Einstein's blackboard.

Albert Einstein.

Friday 15: Pope Pius XI issues the encyclical *Quadrigesimo Anno*, calling for 'justice for the working man.'

Saturday 16: Albert Einstein delivers a lecture in Oxford, after which the blackboard he writes on is preserved for posterity.

The Kentucky Derby is won by Twenty Grand.

Sunday 17: The Nazi party win its first state election in Oldenburg, Germany.

Monday 18: The US Supreme Court rules in Stromberg *v* California that the flying of a communist red flag by a private citizen is not unconstitutional.

Tuesday 19: Joseph Stalin announces the second Five Year Plan for the USSR.

Wednesday 20: The League of Nations issues an official report on world unemployment, estimating it at 20 million people, double that of one year previously.

Thursday 21: Probably the first experimental 'teleconference' takes place as Rotary club speakers are linked with an audience in a different room via closed circuit television in Schenectady, NY.

May 1931

Kipfer and Piccard (wearing padded straw helmets) next to their high-altitude balloon before their record breaking flight.

Friday 22: The provisional government of the new Spanish Republic grants equal freedom to all religious denominations.

Saturday 23: Albert Einstein is awarded an honorary doctorate by the University of Oxford.

Whipsnade Zoo opens in Bedfordshire, England.

Sunday 24: The *Columbia,* the first completely air-conditioned train service, begins between Washington DC and New York City.

Monday 25: The Royal British Legion changes the name of Armistice Day (11 November) to Remembrance Day.

Tuesday 26: Four die when the experimental *Blue Streak* tail-less aeroplane crash lands near Wheaton, Illinois.

Wednesday 27: Professor Auguste Piccard and Paul Kipfer ascend from Augsburg, Germany in a helium balloon, reaching a record altitude of 51,775 ft/9.8 miles (15,781 m).They are the first humans to enter the stratosphere and to observe the curvature of the Earth.

Thursday 28: Three people are killed in clashes between Communists and Nazis in Hagen, Germany.

Friday 29: The Vatican makes a formal protest to the Italian government over recent anti-Papal protests in Rome.

Saturday 30: Daredevil William 'Red' Hill makes his third trip over Niagra Falls in a barrel.

William 'Red' Hill in his diving barrel.

Sunday 31: 200 people are rescued when the ocean liner SS *Harvard* is wrecked in fog at Point Arguello, California.

June
1931

Monday 1: All aristocratic titles are abolished by the provisional Spanish Republican government.

Tuesday 2: The death penalty for pregnant women convicted of murder is abolished in the United Kingdom.

Tommy Armour.

Wednesday 3: Salvador Dali's painting *The Persistence of Memory* is exhibited for the first time at a show in Paris.

Cameronian wins the Epsom Derby.

Thursday 4: The Spanish government seizes 1600 churches, cathedrals and castles claiming them as 'historic and artistic monuments'.

Friday 5: Tommy Armour (USA) beats Jose Jurado of Argentina to win the British Open Men's Golf tournament.

Saturday 6: The USSR government opens the Temlag gulag in Mordovia.

Sunday 7: The Dogger Bank Earthquake, the largest on record (6.1) to hit England, causes damage in many north-eastern towns; tremors are felt as far south as London.

Monday 8: The British colonial administration in Jerusalem grants ownership of the Western Wall to Muslims, with Jews allowed access at all times.

A British policeman at the Western Wall, Jerusalem.

Tuesday 9: The submarine HMS *Poseidon* sinks to 130ft (40m) after colliding with a merchant ship off the Chinese coast. 21 men die but 31 are able to escape, some by using Davis oxygen rebreather equipment.

The comedian Jackie Mason is born in Sheboygan, Wisconsin.

The comedian Jackie Mason is born on 9 June.

Wednesday 10: Germany's Schienenzeppelin high speed train sets a new speed record of 142 mph (230km/h) between Hamburg and Berlin.

Thursday 11: Police in San Francisco begin an investigation into the recruitment of schoolchildren into the Communist Party.

Friday 12: Aviator Amelia Earhart calls off her attempt to cross the Atlantic in an autogyro (a prototype helicopter) when her craft crashes near Abilene, Kansas.

June 1931

Britain's Sir Henry 'Tim' Birkin and Lord Howe celebrate winning Le Mans.

Saturday 13: Paul Doumer becomes President of France.

Sunday 14: Britain's Lord Howe and Sir Henry Birkin win the Le Mans endurance motor race.

Monday 15: The US temperance and women's rights campaigner Anna Adams Gordon dies aged 77.

Tuesday 16: The Bank of England extends a loan of 150 million Schillings to Austria as its banking system and government faces collapse.

Wednesday 17: US President Hoover dedicates the newly remodelled tomb of Abraham Lincoln at Springfield, Illinois.

Thursday 18: Italy's dictator Benito Mussolini makes his famous speech on totalitarianism: 'Everything within the state, nothing outside the state, nothing against the state'.

Friday 19: The first solar or photovoltaic cell goes into commercial use, as a door opening device in West Haven, Connecticut.

Saturday 20: US President Hoover announces a one year moratorium on all Allied war debts owed to the USA, provided they offer the same terms to Germany.

Sunday 21: The best-selling western author Zane Grey is summonsed by US revenue officials over $103,923 in unpaid taxes.

Monday 22: A year-long trial of the Mafia in Sicily ends with 124 mobsters being sent to jail.

Tuesday 23: Wiley Post and Harold Gatty begin their record-breaking flight around the world in a Lockheed Vega from Roosevelt Field, Long Island, NY.

Wednesday 24: The golfer Billy Caspar is born in San Diego, California (died 2015).

Wiley Post and Harold Gatty.

June 1931

Germany and the USSR extend their Treaty of Berlin neutrality pact.

Thursday 25: As the European banking crisis worsens, French, British and American banks give a major loan to Germany's struggling Reichsbank.

Friday 26: *Dracula* star Bela Lugosi of Hungary becomes a US citizen.

The 'beatnik' writer and philosopher Colin Wilson (*The Outsider*) is born in Leicester, England (died 2013).

Saturday 27: Probably the most short-lived country in history, the Republic of Galicia, is created. It lasts only a few hours before Spain's central government re-imposes its rule.

Pope Pius XI.

Sunday 28: Socialist parties win the largest share of the vote in Spain's general election.

Monday 29: Pope Pius XI publishes the encyclical *Non Abbiamo Bisogno*, which condemns fascism.

Tuesday 30: Over 400 people are thought to have died in a heatwave across the US midwest, where temperatures have been over 100F for a week.

July
1931

Wednesday 1: US aviators Wiley Post and Harold Gatty complete their round-the-world flight in a record 8 days 16 hours.

Thursday 2: The German serial killer Peter Kurten is executed by guillotine.

A fistfight breaks out in Britain's House of Commons as a Scottish radical member, John McGovern, refuses to stop speaking.

Friday 3: Max Schmeling retains the World Heavyweight boxing title when he knocks out Young Stribling in Cleveland, Ohio.

The Wimbledon tennis championship is won by Sidney Wood (USA) and Cilley Aussem (Germany).

Saturday 4: A monument to US President Woodrow Wilson is unveiled in Poznan, Poland; it is destroyed by the Nazis in 1939.

Sunday 5: Anti-Chinese rioting breaks out in Pyongyang, Korea; 127 Chinese are killed.

Monday 6: Actor Rudy Vallee marries actress Fay Webb in West Orange, New Jersey.

July 1931

Tuesday 7: US President Hoover announces a 'general disarmament conclave' for the Allied and Central Powers nations.

Wednesday 8: A Civil War bomb explodes and destroys a barn at Camden, Arkansas. The farmer, Hugh Proffitt, states he thought it was a 'dud' and that his children had played with it for years.

Kaye Don.

Thursday 9: Kaye Don (Ireland) sets a water speed record of 110.22 mph in *Miss England* on Lake Garda, Italy.

Friday 10: Norway claims eastern Greenland and names it Erik the Red's Land.

Mel Ott baseball card.

Saturday 11: The film *Smart Money* starring Edward G Robinson and James Cagney is released in the USA.

Sunday 12: Melvin (Mel) Ott of the New York Giants becomes, at 22, the youngest baseball player to hit 100 career home runs.

Monday 13: Germany's Danatbank collapses, sparking a nationwide bank run; all banks are closed for 48 hours.

Tuesday 14: All Hungarian banks are closed for three days to prevent contagion from the German collapse.

Wednesday 15: The thriller writer Clive Cussler is born in Aurora, Illinois (died 2020).

Thursday 16: A bomb is discovered in St Peter's basilica in Rome; it is removed and explodes harmlessly in a nearby field.

Friday 17: Police clash with communists in riots in several German cities.

Saturday 18: Germany introduces strict foreign currency controls.

Sunday 19: 1800 pints of bootleg whisky are seized in FBI raids across Phoenix, Arizona.

Monday 20: Representatives of Great Britain, the United States, and other countries meet in London to discuss aid to Germany.

Tuesday 21: Mr A. A, of Chicago, is announced as having the shortest surname in the USA.

Wednesday 22: Sir Ernest Hotson, Governor of Bombay, survives an assassination attempt when a bullet fired by an Indian nationalist bounces off the metal stud on his wallet.

Joseph Rutherford, leader of the Jehova's Witnesses.

Thursday 23: The London conference on aid to Germany ends with the announcement of a one year moratorium on Germany's debt repayments.

Friday 24: HM King Alfonso XIII of Spain abdicates while in exile in France.

Saturday 25: 17 people die as a heatwave hits the southwestern USA, with temperatures reaching 118F (48C).

Sunday 26: Members of the Bible Student Movement rename their denomination 'Jehovah's Witnesses.'

July 1931

Monday 27: Ramsay MacDonald becomes the first British Prime Minister to visit Germany since the Great War.

Tuesday 28: A pretender to the British throne calling himself 'King Anthony the First' is arrested in Birmingham after a disruptive public campaign to replace HM King George V.

Wednesday 29: The playwright George Bernard Shaw meets Joseph Stalin in Moscow.

British Prime Minister Ramsay Macdonald (left) and Foreign Secretary Arthur Henderson arrive in Berlin.

Thursday 30: Owen Phillips, 1st Baron Kylsant, is sentenced to a year in prison for defrauding the Royal Mail (Rex *v* Kylsant).

Friday 31: Following his meeting with Stalin, George Bernard Shaw describes himself as a 'confirmed communist' and the Soviet leader as a 'most honest and able man'.

August
1931

Saturday 1: The Douglas-RD 'Dolphin' flying boat goes into service with the US Navy.

Sunday 2: Catalonia votes overwhelmingly for independence from Spain in a provincial referendum.

Monday 3: Three black protestors are killed in clashes with police in Chicago in rioting following an eviction case.

Tuesday 4: Dr Daniel Hale Williams, heart surgery pioneer and founder of Chicago's Provident Hospital, dies aged 75.

Wednesday 5: German banks re-introduce regular transactions following the country's financial collapse on 13 July.

A Douglas-RD Dolphin.

August 1931

Poster for *Huckleberry Finn*.

Thursday 6: The traditional jazz musician Bix Beiderbecke dies aged 28.

Friday 7: The comedy film *Huckleberry Finn*, starring Jackie Coogan, is released in the USA.

Saturday 8: The US First Lady, Mrs Herbert Hoover, launches the *Akron*, the world's largest helium airship.

Sunday 9: 16 people are killed in communist-led rioting in Berlin.

Monday 10: Germany's communist newspaper *The Red Flag* is banned for two weeks by the police following Sunday's disturbances.

Tuesday 11: The Hoover Moratorium, a ten year suspension of Germany's war debt repayments, is signed into law in London.

Wednesday 12: The US Army School of Nursing set up in 1918 closes, with nurse training transferred to civilian hospitals.

Thursday 13: Mahatma Gandhi cancels his attendance at talks with the British government due to dissatisfaction over the progress towards Indian independence.

Friday 14: The composer Carl Nielsen's last major work, *Commotio*, is first performed in public at Aarhus, Denmark.

Saturday 15: Rioting breaks out in Northern Ireland after clashes in County Armagh between loyalists and Irish nationalists.

Sunday 16: Britain's Prime Minister Ramsay MacDonald proposes a national tax increase to relieve unemployment.

Monday 17: 14 people are killed in the worst storms to hit Britain in 25 years, with serious floods in London, Newcastle and Dundee.

The world's largest airship, the US Navy's *Akron*, flies over Manhattan.

Tuesday 18: The 1931 China floods hit their worst point; around 3.7 million people die in what is possibly the worst natural disaster of the century.

Wednesday 19: Government troops in Cuba quell an uprising following fierce hand-to-hand fighting with rebels in Gibara.

Thursday 20: The Spanish government bans churches from selling property.

The boxing promoter Don King is born in Cleveland, Ohio.

August 1931

Manfred von Ardenne demonstrates his television and cathode ray tube.

Friday 21: The first fully electronic television set is demonstrated by inventor Manfred von Ardenne to the public at the Berlin Radio Show.

Saturday 22: The US Navy's Asiatic Fleet is mobilised to give assistance to the Chinese cities stricken by recent floods.

Sunday 23: Senior FBI officers defend the use of female undercover agents in Prohibition raids following an attempt to ban their employment on the front line.

Monday 24: Britain's Labour government under Ramsay MacDonald collapses and is replaced by a coalition of Labour, Liberal and Conservative members.

Tuesday 25: Aviator Charles Lindbergh and his wife Anne land in Tokyo after completing a 7000 mile journey from New York.

Wednesday 26: Portuguese government troops put down a revolt after fierce fighting in the capital, Lisbon.

Thursday 27: The world's biggest flying boat, the Dornier Do X, arrives in New York at the end of a 10 month round-the-world trip.

Friday 28: Britain's Labour Party votes out Ramsay MacDonald as leader, replacing him with Arthur Henderson.

Saturday 29: The serial killer Harry Powers, who murdered several women he met through 'lonely hearts' columns, is arrested in Quiet Dell, West Virginia.

Sunday 30: The infamous mobster and bootlegger Mickey Duffy is shot dead by rival gangsters in Atlantic City, New Jersey.

Monday 31: A peace accord is signed between the Vatican and Italy's Fascist government after weeks of anti-clerical violence.

The Dornier Do-X flying boat arrives in New York.

September 1931

Bing Crosby.

Tuesday 1: The Chilean Navy mutinies at Coquimbo.

Wednesday 2: The singer Bing Crosby starts his first solo radio series on CBS.

Thursday 3: PG Wodehouse's comic novel *If I Were You* is published.

Friday 4: Pilot Jimmy Doolittle sets a US transcontinental flight record of 11 hours 16 minutes.

Saturday 5: Glasgow Celtic footballer John Thomson, 22, is fatally injured during a tackle in a match against Rangers at Ibrox Stadium.

Sunday 6: Salary cuts are announced for all British government employees along with reductions to unemployment benefit.

Monday 7: The Second Round Table Conference on Indian independence opens in London; Mahatma Gandhi reverses his previous decision not to attend.

Tuesday 8: Communist agitators attempt to invade Britain's Parliament as MPs vote to cut unemployment benefit.

Wednesday 9: An air-sea rescue search for aviators Don Moyle and Cecil Allen begins, after they go missing on a Japan-USA flight attempt. They are eventually discovered safe in Nome, Alaska, on 21 September.

Thursday 10: 2,500 people are killed when a hurricane hits British Honduras.

Friday 11: The sale of Britain's R100 airship is announced, after its grounding following the crash of its sister ship R101 in 1930.

Saturday 12: Mahatma Gandhi arrives in London for the Round Table conference on Indian independence; he stays in an East End working mens' hostel where he is greeted by large crowds.

Sunday 13: Flight Lieutenant George Stainforth wins the Schneider Trophy for Great Britain, setting the air speed record at 386.1mph.

Gandhi is mobbed by enthusiastic crowds in London's East End.

September 1931

Monday 14: The second Round Table Conference on Indian independence opens in London.

Tuesday 15: Around 1000 sailors of the Royal Navy mutiny at Invergordon over pay cuts.

Wednesday 16: The Invergordon Mutiny is put down after the government compromises on pay cuts; the ringleaders are jailed and 200 sailors are dismissed from the service.

Thursday 17: RCA Victor introduces the Long Playing (LP) record (33 ⅓ rpm) but it fails to catch on due to high costs.

Friday 18: The Japanese army plants a bomb on the Japanese owned South Manchuria Railway in China, as a pretext for a Japanese invasion of Manchuria.

Saturday 19: The Japanese invasion of Manchuria begins.

Charlie Chaplin meets the Gandhi family in London.

Buster Keaton.

Sunday 20: Britain decides to take the Pound Sterling off the Gold Standard.

Monday 21: Legislation to remove the Pound Sterling from the Gold Standard is rushed through Britain's Parliament in a single day.

Tuesday 22: Charlie Chaplin meets Mahatma Gandhi, who is in London for the Round Table Conference on Indian independence.

Wednesday 23: The Soviet Union makes a formal protest to Japan over its invasion of Manchuria.

Thursday 24: The US Navy's flagship dirigible the *Akron* makes its first night flight.

Friday 25: Cheering crowds greet Mahatma Gandhi when he tours the cotton mills of Lancashire in the north of England.

Saturday 26: The comedy film *Sidewalks of New York* starring Buster Keaton is released.

Sunday 27: Norway, Sweden and Egypt abandon the Gold Standard.

Monday 28: Denmark goes off the Gold Standard.

Tuesday 29: Demonstrators clash with police in London as new figures show unemployment has reached a record 2.8 million.

Wednesday 30: Mahatma Gandhi meets with Britain's Prime Minister, Ramsay MacDonald.

October
1931

Thursday 1: The world's biggest hotel at this date, the rebuilt Waldorf Astoria, opens in New York City.

Friday 2: A second night of rioting by unemployed protesters takes place in Glasgow, Scotland.

Saturday 3: The Scottish grocery store magnate and tea merchant Sir Thomas Lipton dies aged 83.

Sunday 4: The cartoon detective hero Dick Tracy first appears, in the *Detroit Mirror.*

Monday 5: Clyde Pangborn and Hugh Herndon Jr of the USA make the first non-stop trans-Pacific flight, from Japan to Washington State in 41 hours.

Tuesday 6: The notorious gangster Al Capone goes on trial for tax evasion.

Wednesday 7: 14 people are injured when unemployed protesters clash with police in Manchester, England, after trying to invade the city's council chambers.

Left: Al Capone.

Thursday 8: One of the earliest TV programmes in the USA, *Piano Lessons* with G Aldo Rendegger, is first broadcast on the experimental station WCBS-TV in New York.

Friday 9: The League of Nations announces it will hold crisis talks on the Sino-Japanese conflict in Manchuria.

Saturday 10: The St Louis Cardinals beat the Philadelphia Athletics 4-2 to win the USA's Baseball World Series.

Sunday 11: Germany's radical right-wing parties combine to form the Harzburg Front.

The statue of Christ the Redeemer, Rio de Janeiro, is inaugurated on 12 October.

Monday 12: The statue of Christ the Redeemer, Rio de Janeiro, is inaugurated.

Tuesday 13: The Noel Coward play *Cavalcade* premieres in London.

Wednesday 14: A new radical and anti-clerical Spanish government takes over under President Manuel Azana.

Thursday 15: The Jerome Kern musical *The Cat and the Fiddle* opens on Broadway.

Left: advert for the Waldorf Astoria hotel.

October 1931

Friday 16: The notorious Phoenix murderess Winnie Ruth Judd kills two female friends; she is later caught after attempting to remove their bodies in trunks on a railway train.

Saturday 17: Gangster Al Capone is reportedly in tears as a Chicago jury convicts him of tax evasion. He is sentenced to 11 years in prison.

Mickey Mantle.

Sunday 18: The US inventor Thomas Alva Edison dies aged 84.

Monday 19: The espionage writer John le Carré (*Tinker Tailor Soldier Spy*) is born in Dorset, England.

Tuesday 20: The legendary New York Yankees baseball player Mickey Mantle is born in Spavinaw, Oklahoma (died 1995).

Wednesday 21: The lights of the White House in Washington, DC and buildings across the USA are put out for one minute in commemoration of Thomas Edison, who died on Sunday.

Thursday 22: The League of Nations issues a statement ordering Japan to withdraw from Manchuria by 16 November.

Friday 23: Winnie Ruth Judd is arrested for the infamous Trunk Murders of 16 October in Phoenix, Arizona.

Saturday 24: The George Washington Bridge between Manhattan and New Jersey is opened.

Sunday 25: Large scale anti-British rioting breaks out in Nicosia, Cyprus.

Monday 26: The play *Mourning Becomes Electra* by Eugene O'Neill premieres on Broadway.

Tuesday 27: The coalition National Government under Ramsay MacDonald wins the British General Election.

Wednesday 28: Commercial retail prices in the USSR are lowered by 30% as part of the Five Year Plan.

Thursday 29: Married couple Betty and Babe Fox begin a 100 hour 'dance marathon' on a platform perched on a 50-foot pole in Texarcana, Texas.

Friday 30: The American Aid Society in Paris announces a large increase in destitute US expats, mostly artists, requesting assistance.

Saturday 31: Fifteen countries agree to a one year arms production embargo imposed by the League of Nations.

The last Ford Model A car is produced on 31 October.

November
1931

Sunday 1: Divers salvage $130,000 in bullion from the wreck of the SS *Colombia* which sank off the California coast in September.

Monday 2: The first synthetic rubber, DuPrene (neoprene), is launched by DuPont.

Tuesday 3: Germany bans all large outdoor gatherings due to worsening violence between communists and fascists.

David Lloyd George.

Wednesday 4: David Lloyd George resigns as leader of Britain's Liberal Party and is replaced by Sir Herbert Samuel.

Thursday 5: Mahatma Gandhi meets HM King George V at a Buckingham Palace reception. Gandhi causes a sensation by wearing only a loincloth and sandals for the event.

Friday 6: Mahatma Gandhi meets the playwright and social reformer George Bernard Shaw in London.

Pu Yi, the last Emperor of China.

Saturday 7: The Chinese Soviet Republic in Jiangxi is established under Mao Zedong.

Sunday 8: US, French and Italian soldiers are turned out to protect expatriates as rioting breaks out in Tientsin, China.

Monday 9: The boxing film *The Champ* starring Wallace Beery is released in the USA.

Tuesday 10: Pu Yi, the exiled last Emperor of China, accepts the offer of the throne of Japanese occupied Manchuria.

Wednesday 11: The District of Columbia War Memorial in Washington, DC, is dedicated by President Hoover.

Thursday 12: The Abbey Road recording studios in London are opened by the composer Sir Edward Elgar.

Friday 13: Hattie Wyatt Caraway becomes the first female US Senator.

Saturday 14: Coin making in Canada becomes independent of Great Britain as the Royal Canadian Mint is opened.

Sunday 15: The Bayonne Bridge connecting New Jersey with Staten Island is opened.

Senator Caraway.

November 1931

Monday 16: Britain's R100 airship, grounded since the crash of its sister ship the R101 in 1930, is sold for scrap.

Tuesday 17: The Svirlag gulag (forced labour camp) near Leningrad is opened by the Soviet government.

Wednesday 18: Adolf Hitler holds talks with Princess Hermine, wife of Germany's exiled Kaiser Wilhelm, to court favour with monarchists.

Thursday 19: The US government announces it will not support League of Nations sanctions against Japan over the invasion of Manchuria.

Friday 20: The British luxury car maker Bentley is bought by Rolls Royce.

Saturday 21: The horror film *Frankenstein* starring Colin Clive and Boris Karloff is released in the USA.

Britain's R100 airship is scrapped on 16 November.

Sunday 22: *The Grand Canyon Suite* by US composer Ferde Grofe is performed for the first time, in Chicago.

Monday 23: The journalists Walter Kreiser and Carl von Ossietzky are sentenced to 18 months' imprisonment for revealing Germany's plans to build a secret air force in breach of the Treaty of Versailles.

Tuesday 24: Four people die as severe blizzards hit Colorado.

Wednesday 25: Secret plans for a Nazi takeover of Germany in the event of a communist uprising are revealed; senior Nazis deny any involvement.

Thursday 26: China and Japan agree to take part in League of Nations peace talks over the war in Manchuria.

Friday 27: Six Europeans are killed in the expatriate area of Tsientsin, China, as fighting increases between Chinese and occupying Japanese forces.

Saturday 28: The actor Tom Mix, Hollywood's first screen cowboy, is reported to be on the mend after being near to death with peritonitis.

Sunday 29: Tax statistics show the USA has 19,688 millionaires, half the amount it had before the Wall Street Crash of 1929.

Monday 30: The Chinese government accepts the League of Nations' proposals for a buffer zone between China and Japanese-occupied Manchuria.

December
1931

Tuesday 1: The second Round Table conference on Indian independence ends in a stalemate due to conflicting Hindu and Muslim demands.

Wednesday 2: US scientist Prof Robert Andrews Millikan announces he has found a way to split the atom; he is beaten to it by Britain's Ernest Rutherford in 1932.

Thursday 3: The pain reliever Alka Seltzer is launched by the Dr Miles Medical Company.

Friday 4: Pilot Lowell R Bayles, 31, is killed attempting to break the world air speed record when his plane crashes near Detroit, Michigan.

Saturday 5: Communists demolish Moscow's Cathedral of Christ the Saviour and begin to build in its place the Palace of the Soviets, which is never completed. The cathedral is rebuilt in 2000.

Sunday 6: The trial of Harry Powers, the 'Lonely Hearts' killer who targetted his victims through the small ads, begins in Clarksburg, West Virginia. He is sentenced to death on 10 December.

Monday 7: The drama film *Arrowsmith* starring Ronald Colman and Myrna Loy premieres in New York City.

Tuesday 8: US President Herbert Hoover gives his State of the Union Address, outlining his government's efforts to tackle the Depression.

Wednesday 9: The new Spanish Constitution, with strict controls on the Roman Catholic church, goes into effect.

Thursday 10: The USA's Jane Addams and Nicholas Murray Butler are awarded the Nobel Peace Prize.

Below: The Cathedral of Christ the Saviour, Moscow, is destroyed on 5 December. It is eventually rebuilt 69 years later.

Friday 11: The Statute of Westminster is passed, giving legislative equality to the British Dominions of Australia, Canada, South Africa, New Zealand and the Irish Free State.

Saturday 12: Work on the *Queen Mary* ocean liner in Glasgow is suspended for two years as the company runs out of money.

Mahatma Gandhi meets with Benito Mussolini in Rome.

Actor Lionel Blair is born in Montreal, Canada.

Sunday 13: The British politician Winston Churchill is hospitalised for eight days after being knocked down by a speeding car in New York City.

December 1931

Monday 14: Prohibition agents make a series of raids on high-class drinking clubs in Atlantic City, New Jersey, seizing property worth $20,000.

Chiang Kai Shek.

Tuesday 15: Chiang Kai Shek resigns as President of China over criticism of his nationalist views.

Wednesday 16: The Iron Front, a paramilitary organisation defending liberal democracy, is formed in Germany.

Thursday 17: Japan goes off the Gold Standard.

Friday 18: The notorious mobster Jack 'Legs' Diamond is killed in a gangland slaying in Albany, New York.

Saturday 19: Joseph Lyons becomes Prime Minister of Australia as the United Australia Party wins the Federal elections.

Sunday 20: French Prime Minister Pierre Laval announces that France will never accept recent US proposals to cancel Germany's war debts.

Monday 21: Japanese troops launch an offensive at Chinchow, Manchuria, claiming they are not violating the League of Nations peace terms but 'clearing the area of bandits'.

Joseph Lyons, Prime Minister of Australia.

Tuesday 22: The roof of the Vatican Library collapses, killing five people and destroying 800 books.

Wednesday 23: The administrators of the US Young Plan for German war repayments announce that Germany will not be able to meet its obligations in 1932.

Thursday 24: Unemployed protestors riot in the Montmartre district of Paris, causing damage to cafes and demanding 'work and bread'.

Friday 25: The first New York Metropolitan Opera radio broadcast, *Hansel and Gretel* by Engelbert Humperdinck, is made on NBC.

Saturday 26: The spy film *Mata Hari* starring Greta Garbo is released.

Melvil Dewey, inventor of the Dewey Decimal System of library classification, dies aged 80.

Sunday 27: The statue of Eros is returned to Piccadilly Circus, London, after removal in 1922 for the construction of an underground station.

Monday 28: Huge crowds turn out in Bombay to greet Mahatma Gandhi as he returns to India from his European tour.

Tuesday 29: Japanese troops withdraw from the League of Nations' buffer zone in Chinchow.

Greta Garbo and Ramon Navarro in *Mata Hari.*

December 1931

Wednesday 30: The paramilitary wing of Germany's Nazi party, the SS, makes it mandatory for all members to be able to trace their German ancestry back to 1750.

Thursday 31: A manhunt begins in Canada for Albert Johnson, the 'mad trapper' who attempted to murder a Royal Canadian Mounted Police officer. He is eventually killed in a shoot out in 1932.

The horror film *Dr Jekyl and Mr Hyde* starring Fredric March is released.

Fredric March and Holmes Herbert in *Dr. Jekyll and Mr. Hyde*, released on 31 December.

Other titles from Montpelier Publishing:

A Little Book of Limericks:
Funny Rhymes for all the Family
ISBN 9781511524124

Scottish Jokes: A Wee Book of
Clean Caledonian Chuckles
ISBN 9781495297366

The Old Fashioned Joke Book:
Gags and Funny Stories
ISBN 9781514261989

Non-Religious Funeral Readings:
Philosophy and Poetry for Secular
Services
ISBN 9781500512835

Large Print Jokes: Hundreds of
Gags in Easy-to-Read Type
ISBN 9781517775780

**Spiritual Readings for Funerals
and Memorial Services**
ISBN 9781503379329

Victorian Murder: True Crimes,
Confessions and Executions
ISBN 9781530296194

Large Print Prayers: A Prayer for
Each Day of the Month
ISBN 9781523251476

**A Little Book of Ripping Riddles
and Confounding Conundrums**
ISBN 9781505548136

Vinegar uses: over 150 ways to use
vinegar
ISBN 9781512136623

Large Print Wordsearch:
100 Puzzles in Easy-to-Read Type
ISBN 9781517638894

The Pipe Smoker's Companion
ISBN 9781500441401

The Book of Church Jokes
ISBN 9781507620632

Bar Mitzvah Notebook
ISBN 9781976007781

Jewish Jokes
ISBN 9781514845769

Large Print Address Book
ISBN 9781539820031

How to Cook Without a Kitchen:
Easy, Healthy and Low-Cost Meals
9781515340188

Large Print Birthday Book
ISBN 9781544670720

Retirement Jokes
ISBN 9781519206350

Take my Wife: Hilarious Jokes of
Love and Marriage
ISBN 9781511790956

Welsh Jokes: A Little Book of
Wonderful Welsh Wit
ISBN 9781511612241

1001 Ways to Save Money: Thrifty
Tips for the Fabulously Frugal!
ISBN 9781505432534

Available online at Amazon.com